COOKING WI...

ESSENTIAL OILS

Increase the appeal of food with just one drop.

b a s m a t i

For more articles on Earth-friendly lifestyle and holistic health & wellness, visit our website, www.basmati.com. You'll find articles on yoga; meditation; essential oils; Ayurveda; recipes that are vegan, vegetarian, or gluten-free; and more. You can also use our "Find" feature to locate a yoga studio or a wellness practitioner near you.

Looking for more healthy, seasonal recipes? Visit www.basmati.com/tags/recipes.

Information published by basmati.com is no substitute for medical advice. Please consult your health care provider before beginning any new regimen. For more information, please visit our disclaimer page at https://basmati.com/disclaimer.

basmati

Published by basmati

www.basmati.com

editors@basmati.com

ISBN 978-1980246350

Table of Contents

Introduction

Increase the appeal of food with just one drop.

This book is designed to introduce you to the concept of adding essential oils to your food. When used in moderation, essential oils can enhance the flavor of new dishes and add complex nuances to old favorites. Combining the power of essential oils with the ancient wisdom of Ayurveda opens up even more opportunities to treat your body to healthy, healing eating. Ayurveda recommends seasonal eating, and this book is designed with the three Ayurveda seasons in mind (**Spring**, **Summer**, and **Fall/Winter**). You'll find some extra categories (**Sips** and **Sweets**), but they too give nod to the benefits of eating ingredients when they're in season. Ayurveda also advises mindful eating: truly focusing on your food and eating with gratitude and intention. You'll find other Ayurveda lifestyle advice sprinkled throughout this book, too.

The recipes in this book are vegan, with the exception of a couple that call for honey (try substituting agave, maple syrup, or stevia) and the Spiced Pumpkin Soup with Chickpeas, which calls for Greek yogurt. However, many of the recipes recommend options to add meat or seafood or provide other dietary choices (such as using butter, ghee, or oil).

The pure, organic, food grade essential oils you should use in these recipes can be expensive. With that in mind, you can make all of the recipes except two with only three different essential oils: lemongrass, cinnamon bark, and black pepper. (The other two recipes call for rosemary, lemon, and peppermint essential oils.) If you don't have a specific essential oil or you're not comfortable ingesting it for whatever reason, you can make the recipes with the corresponding ingredient. If a recommendation isn't given in the recipe, experiment! Remember that essential oils are very concentrated, so one drop might equal 1/4 or 1/2 teaspoon of a dried spice.

If you just skim this section, at least take a look at **The Basics: Getting Started**, which tells you a few things you need to know about cooking with essential oils—such as use them in moderation; they're strong!

The Basics: Getting Started

Cooking with essential oils requires a bit of care.

1. Use only pure, organic, food grade essential oils.

When buying essential oils, always look for quality; the best are pure and organic—and make sure they are food grade.

2. Use essential oils in moderation.

Because they're so concentrated, you only need a little. You should only add a drop or two to your food. Start with one, and add more if needed. You also shouldn't ingest essential oils too often, as they can be difficult for your liver to process in high doses.

3. Use nonreactive utensils and containers.

Always use nonreactive utensils and containers when measuring and mixing— glass is best, since plastic can absorb the essential oils.

4. Don't expose essential oils to high heat.

In order to preserve nutrients, anytime you cook with essential oils, add them after you've removed the food from any heat source. High heat diminishes their nutritional properties. Essential oils also work well in cold foods like smoothies, nut milks, jellies, non-alcoholic spritzers, dips, and icing.

The Essential Oil Controversy

Essential oils add interesting taste and energy to food, due to concentration and the way the flavor is distributed, but ingesting them is a controversial topic, and a personal choice. Opinions abound on what is safe essential oil usage. One extreme view is that oils have too many unknowns due to lack of research and are, thus, potentially dangerous. Others may use them daily in high amounts: applying them undiluted on the skin while diffusing them all day long into the air and even drinking some daily in water. It's likely the real answer lies somewhere between the two extremes.

Regardless, essential oils are highly concentrated and super strong. For example, it takes about sixteen pounds of thyme to create one ounce of thyme essential oil. This means more work for your liver, which is why essential oils should always be used in moderation. And some people choose not to ingest them at all. (Read one writer's opinion on why you shouldn't put lemon essential oil in your water at https://basmati.com/2017/08/22/essential-oil-essentials-what-safe-oil-usage.) Anyone with liver or kidney problems should also avoid ingesting essential oils.

Substitutions

If you choose not to add essential oils to your recipes (or don't have the required essential oil), you can still make these delicious dishes. Just use the corresponding ingredient—but you'll need to add much more of the dried or fresh spice than you would the essential oil. For example, one drop of black pepper essential oil is roughly equivalent to 1/4 teaspoon of ground black pepper. You might have to experiment with different ingredients to find the right amount. And remember that essential oils are added after the dish is removed from heat in order to preserve their nutritional properties, but if you're using the spice version, you'll want to add it earlier in the recipe, with the rest of the herbs and spices.

FAQ with Samantha Lee Wright

To learn more about the magic of essential oils, I turned to essential oil educator Samantha Lee Wright, host of *The Essential Oil Revolution*, the top-rated podcast on the subject. (Try her Essential Lemon Peppermint Water recipe in this book!)

What Are Essential Oils?

"Essential oils are concentrated, volatile extracts from trees and the petals, flowers, rinds, grasses, leaves, and roots of plants," explained Wright. Although most of us don't realize it, essential oils have long been used in the concoctions created by the food, cosmetics, and medical industries. Essential oils are incredibly versatile and can be used in home for personal care, cleaning, physical and emotional wellbeing, nutritional support, and cooking. Yes, cooking!

Why Should I Eat Essential Oils?

In addition to imparting great flavor, Wright said health benefits, convenience, and economy are some of the reasons she loves cooking with essential oils. We're just beginning to understand their nutritional value. They contain vitamins, nutrients, and trace elements. Studies indicate many of them boast an extraordinary level of antioxidants, some aid digestion, and they all seem to have some psychological effect on us. They're biochemically harmonic with the human body, which means they enter and leave it with great efficiency, leaving no toxins behind, unlike many other flavor enhancers and mood stimulants. All of this comes in a tiny bottle with a long shelf life that transports easily and can be enjoyed year-round, even when its fresh counterparts are out of season. And although the best essential oils might seem pricey, their intense concentration makes them less expensive than using fresh herbs, flowers, and fruit.

Which Essential Oils Should I Eat?

Essential oils for culinary use fall into four categories: herbs, spices, citrus, and flowers. Some of Wright's favorites include peppermint (for brownies), orange (for waffles and smoothies), and black pepper (on roasted vegetables). Another favorite is lemongrass. "It seems like I'm putting it in everything right now," she said. "It's great in soup, rice, and chicken tikka masala."

Since essential oils are volatile and highly concentrated, handle them mindfully. Good cooking is all about balance; essential oils should enhance a dish, not overpower it. Start with one drop, and then taste and adjust in small increments. Flavor and aroma can vary based on brand and even in different batches, so experimentation through tasting is key. Also, introducing an oil to a food after you've removed it from its heat source is best; high heat diminishes an essential oil's nutritional properties. And of course, use only pure, organic essential oils from a source that you trust. The choice to ingest essential oils remains a controversial topic that hinges on quality and purity. Supporting companies that manufacture quality products is good for your health and encourages further research into nature's fragrant apothecary.

Samantha Lee Wright is the host of The Essential Oil Revolution. *Each week she interviews the world's top experts about essential oils, sharing hundreds of recipes and different ways to use them. Her favorite guests have included chefs, food experts, and oil-inspired restaurant owners. The* Essential Oil Revolution *is freely available on iTunes and Stitcher.*

Spring

Herb Salad with Lemongrass Dressing

No-Bake Bliss Bites

refreshing & satisfying

Do the gorgeous blooms of spring turn you into a sneezing, sniffling, itchy-eyed mess? Food can help.

We were sitting by the pool enjoying one of the warmer days of spring when a dear allergy pill-popping friend noticed that I'm allergy-free. I had suffered from mild seasonal allergies since childhood, even after years of enjoying numerous other benefits of a healthy lifestyle. So what had changed? Over the last year, I had begun to shift my diet with the seasons. My idea was to live more in harmony with nature, and my allergies disappeared in the process.

Although I've been eating a real food diet for more than 20 years, I managed to remain largely oblivious to seasonal foods. Shopping at the grocery store—where food is shipped in from all over the world—encourages that kind of obliviousness. And let's face it: when the cruel New York winter gets you down, strawberries in the grocery store can be like a beacon from some dreamy, warm, faraway place. But when those gorgeous sirens call, there's good reason to wait a few more months.

Why Eat Seasonally?

The first reason to eat seasonally is taste. Think about it: how do you feel after a stuffy long-haul flight? Like us humans, food is simply better when it's not crammed and shipped long distances. The other reasons are couched in the old idea that seasonal foods are meant to support the body's needs at a particular time. For example, in fall-winter Ayurveda favors foods that are heavy, high-fat, and high-protein, such as meat, nuts, and seeds, which warm and balance the accumulation of dryness in the body. To move us gracefully out of the internally focused time of winter, when spring rolls around, lighter foods such as bitter greens and berries are suggested. Spring foods are energizing and give the body a fresh start. They cleanse the body of winter build-up and balance moistness, which is particularly helpful when we begin to spend more time outdoors and are exposed to increased dampness and pollen.

When spring is here, I want you to feel refreshed and energized like the little buds that are bursting forth from the earth. So here I present you with a salad that's abundant with the energy of spring herbs and vegetables. Paired with a slightly warming coconut and sesame oil dressing made tangy with a few drops of lemongrass essential oil, this is a great salad during the alternating cold/warm cycles of spring. The inclusion of cashews and sesame seeds makes it surprisingly satisfying, but you could also add tofu, or even chicken, shrimp, or squid, if you're of that persuasion.

These days I'm extolling the benefits of seasonal eating every chance I get. In Ayurveda, it's believed that if you balance the winter's dryness through diet, you'll produce less mucus in the spring, which could very well be the reason I'm not sniffling and sneezing. And since I've been so good and feel so great, I'm going to have a glass of champagne to celebrate, because a little of that is *always* in season.

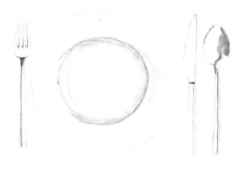

Herb Salad with Lemongrass Dressing

Servings: 4

Ingredients

for the dressing

- 1/4 cup virgin coconut oil (use gentle heat to melt if necessary)
- 2 tablespoons toasted sesame oil
- 3 tablespoons brown rice vinegar
- 2 tablespoons honey (clear honey is easiest to use)
- 1 teaspoon sea salt
- 1 teaspoon finely grated fresh ginger
- 1 garlic clove, minced
- 2 drops food grade lemongrass essential oil

for the salad

- 4 cups shredded cabbage
- 2 cups chopped mixed greens
- 1/3 cup chopped cilantro
- 1/3 cup chopped mint
- 1/3 cup chopped parsley
- 1/2 cup chopped basil
- 1/2 cup spring onions or scallions, thinly sliced
- 1 carrot, cut into thin ribbons
- 1 cup presoaked cashews
- 1/2 cup sesame seeds

Directions

1. Make the dressing by mixing all the ingredients in a nonreactive (preferably glass) container. Cover and shake vigorously until everything is well combined. Set aside.

2. In a large bowl, mix together all the salad elements. Add dressing and toss. Serve immediately.

This on-the-go snack is healthy and delicious—perfect for taking on spring trips or hikes.

Has hunger ever gotten the best of you midflight and led you to eat those things that the airlines pass off as cookies? I set off on a project recently to create a portable snack that I could take on a plane. I had a few prerequisites: it had to be nutritious and treat-like, meaning it had to feel like some kind of reward for getting myself through airport security and onto the plane with my sanity intact. The result? Blissful energy bites, which are sweetish cashew-based snacks. They're rich in nutrients and fiber from dates, heart healthy almonds, and omega-3-rich chia seeds, which means they'll give you energy without the dreadful post-high sluggishness that simple sugar imparts. One of the many things I love about these is they offer an opportunity to use cinnamon bark essential oil. Its deep, perfume-y fragrance works well with sweet flavors, and since this is a no-heat recipe, all the nutrients in the oil remain intact. Cinnamon essential oil is purported to increase immunity—an added bonus when you have to spend time on a stuffy airplane.

Recipe Notes

This recipe is very easy to put together with a food processor. I like presoaking the nuts, which gives them a creamy texture and makes them easier to digest. Soak the cashews in water with a little sea salt for a few hours (no more than six hours or the texture and flavor will suffer). The almonds can be soaked the same way, for about 7 hours. If you'd like to store the nuts after soaking, place them on a baking sheet in a warm oven (no higher than 150° F) for 12-24 hours before keeping them in the refrigerator. If you don't have time for soaking, skip this step, but you might find that you need to use a little more water in the recipe. Also, the dates you choose should be moist and soft. Deglet and Medjool are my preferred varieties because of their great flavor and texture. In my world, dates and roses are perfect partners, so the day I photographed the bites I garnished them with petals. Of course, rose petals are beautiful and they've also been used therapeutically across many cultures.

Cooking with essential oils requires a bit of care. In this recipe, use one drop of oil diluted in water, as instructed below. Not letting too much oil escape from the bottle can be tricky at first. Tipping the bottle with one hand and gently tapping it with the ring finger of your other hand will likely do the trick. If you accidently drop too much oil into the water, drink it and try again (it will taste great). Using too much essential oil will, without doubt, overpower the other ingredients. Diluting the oil in water also encourages even flavor distribution. If you don't have essential oil you can substitute a half teaspoon of cinnamon powder.

These bites are kind of like a healthy version of cookie dough. While they're certainly not diet snacks, they are nutritious and energizing, and they'll satisfy your hunger like nothing on the flight attendant's rolling cart.

No-Bake Bliss Bites

Servings: approximately 12

Ingredients

- 1/4 cup raw presoaked almonds
- 3/4 cup raw, presoaked cashews
- 1 tablespoon coconut oil, melted
- 1 tablespoon chia seeds
- 1/2 cup chopped dates (preferably Medjool)
- 2 tablespoons water
- 1/2 teaspoon pure vanilla extract
- 1/8 teaspoon sea salt
- 1 drop food grade cinnamon bark essential oil (or 1/2 teaspoon ground cinnamon)
- 1/8 cup bitter-sweet chocolate, chopped

Directions

1. Using a food processor, pulse almonds and cashews until very fine crumbs form.

2. Combine water, vanilla extract, salt, and cinnamon bark essential oil in a small glass or other nonreactive bowl, stir, and set aside to allow time for the salt to dissolve.

3. Add coconut oil, chia seeds, and dates to the mixture in the food processor and pulse until smooth. (You might have to stop and scrape down the bowl periodically.) Then add essential oil mixture and pulse again until evenly combined.

4. Transfer the mixture to a small bowl, add chocolate, and mix with a spoon.

5. Form into small balls. Eat immediately or refrigerate.

Summer

Watermelon Gazpacho

Cucumber Noodles with Peanut Sauce

Make this chilled soup with a twist to experience summer in a bowl.

Many years ago, after a few hours on a sweltering beach, my friend and I gathered ourselves and climbed the dunes to a restaurant. It was on the patio there that we two tired, over-sunned, young girls were brought back to life by generous bowls of cool, hearty, earthy gazpacho. Every summer since, when the temperatures soar, I think: soup. And although I love a good tomato gazpacho, that's just the beginning. On hot evenings when the thought of turning the stove on is enough to cause a sweat, there are few dishes more appropriate than watermelon gazpacho. Watermelon is 90% water, so it's unsurprising that this soup is cooling, hydrating, and easy to digest. My rendition is a blend of summer pitta balancing fruits, vegetables, and herbs. Watermelon, tomato, and cucumber are blended with touches of ginger and lemongrass essential oil, and the whole thing is garnished with mint and cilantro. What you end up with is a delicious, effortless soup that pleases both adults and children. Another of its virtues is that it works well for one or a crowd. It can be put together at the last moment, or refrigerated for up to three days. It's ovely on its own, or at the end of a long meal. You can also add crab or shrimp to it for a more ubstantial meal. It's particularly festive when presented in a bowl made of watermelon rind. (I ypically keep my watermelon bowls to a minimal aesthetic, but I've seen quite elaborate ones. If ou'd like to practice your pumpkin carving skills during the summer, this is the activity for you.)

Recipe Notes

Gazpacho is a pleasing reminder that delicious food needn't be complicated. It's hard to go wrong with gazpacho, but using the best, freshest ingredients will make yours great. When selecting most of its ingredients you can rely on sight and smell, but watermelon is a little more challenging. When selecting one, knock on it; if it sounds hollow, it's ripe. When putting the gazpacho together, grate the ginger using a microplane zester before adding it to the food processor so it combines well. And avoid over-blending: the soup should be thick and heavy. If you refrigerate it, be mindful that chilling will suspend the flavors somewhat; taste it again before serving as you might find that you need to adjust the seasoning.

Summer in a Bowl

Watermelon gazpacho tastes like summer in a bowl, for good reason. It's composed of an array of summer produce. In Ayurveda, it's believed that adjusting one's diet and lifestyle in cyclical harmony with the seasons promotes optimal health. Recent research from the Human Microbiome Project found that 90% of the cells that make up the human body are bacteria, viruses, and other microorganisms. Soil microbes change seasonally and show up on produce. Fruits and vegetables are rich in microbes that support our bodies at a particular time, affecting immunity, digestion, mood, energy, weight, and sleep cycles. For example, the summer harvest is abundant in high-carb, low-fat foods that keep us energized during increased time in the sun. These foods tend to be cool, moist, heavy, and oily; they balance the season's hot, light, and dry characteristics.

As a nation, we Americans are mostly ambivalent about chilled soups, which is a shame. If you're at all hesitant, think of chilled soup as a step away from a smoothie, and dive in.

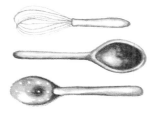

Watermelon Gazpacho

Servings: about 4 cups

Ingredients

for the soup

- 1-1/2 lb. peeled, seeded, and cubed watermelon (about half of a small watermelon)
- 1/2 lb. ripe tomatoes, chopped
- 1 cucumber (approximately 8 ounces), peeled and chopped
- 1/4 cup virgin coconut oil (I like wet-milled/fermented)
- 1 teaspoon fresh ginger, finely grated
- 1 drop food grade lemongrass essential oil
- pinch of sea salt

for the garnish

- fresh coriander, chopped
- fresh mint, chopped
- edible flowers (optional)

Directions

1. Combine all the ingredients in a food processor or blender and purée until well combined but still thick.

2. Garnish with coriander, mint, and edible flowers (if using). Serve immediately or refrigerate for up to three days.

cooling &
hydrating

Keep cool with this dish that features cucumbers—with a twist.

Do you want to naturally help your body stay cool during the hot summer months? If so, eat more cucumbers. The expression "cool as a cucumber" originates from the fact that when on the vine, a cucumber's interior flesh is 20 degrees cooler than the outside temperature, even on a hot day. Cucumbers are, after all, over 90% water. In addition to being cooling, they're also hydrating, particularly when eaten raw.

I've always found it impossible not to love cucumbers, but the recipe I'm sharing here led to many more in my life. It's a beautifully simple, healthy salad that can serve as a full meal. The cucumber's subtle, fresh flavor is combined with peppery bok choy and a tangy peanut sauce. Shrimp is a delicious addition here if you'd like a more substantial meal, but this salad is surprisingly satisfying on its own due to the complexity of the sauce. Either way, this is a wonderful dish for those of us who want to keep our cool, but still like a little spice.

Recipe Notes

When putting this together, I cut the cucumbers into "noodles" with a spiralizer, which makes prepping effortless. Just trim the cucumber's short ends, place it center aligned in the spiralizer, press to secure, turn the handle, and you have cucumber noodles. If you don't have a spiralizer, are great at slicing, or want to *become* great at slicing, try a julienne cut.

Regardless of how it's sliced, I prefer to use the whole vegetable as opposed to peeling it. Remove the peel if you'd like a more elegant dish with a more consistent texture, or if you're using conventional produce. And by all means, serve this immediately after you're done preparing it. Because of the high water content in the cucumbers, it will get soggy if left sitting, and the flavor of the sauce will diminish.

Eating Raw Foods

The ancient system of Ayurveda favors gently cooked foods, except in the summer, when raw is acceptable. Although Julia Child made a great case for cooking cucumbers, it turns out there's interesting scientific reason to eat them and other summer vegetables raw when they're in season. A study published by PLoS One in 2014 found that microbes that digest raw foods are highest in the human gut during the summer.

My innate wisdom is closely intertwined with cucumbers. I must have sensed their soothing effect on my body when, as a child, I devoured generous portions during hot summers. Over time, my food journey developed to include sojourns into emotional eating, nutritionism, dietary dogma, and politics. Then a much-welcomed realization came when the taste of a cucumber reminded me that long before any of that, I possessed the innate wisdom to know what my body needed. Health speaks in a small voice that exists inside of all of us, if we can get quiet and listen.

Cucumber Noodles with Peanut Sauce

Servings: 4

Ingredients

- 1-1/2 pounds seedless cucumbers (such as English, Armenian, or Persian)
- 1/2 pound standard bok choy (or 1 medium baby bok choy for subtle flavor)

for the sauce

- 1/4 cup peanut butter
- 1 tablespoon brown rice vinegar
- 1 tablespoon grated fresh ginger
- 1 tablespoon tamari sauce
- 1 clove garlic, smashed with the back of a large knife
- 1 tablespoon lime juice (about half of a lime)
- 2 teaspoons maple syrup
- 1/4 teaspoon toasted sesame oil
- 1/8 teaspoon five-spice powder
- 1 drop food grade lemongrass essential oil
- pinch of sea salt

for the garnish

- 1/4 cup dried shredded coconut, toasted
- 1/4 cup chopped cilantro
- 3-4 scallions, chopped
- 1/4 cup chopped peanuts
- 1/4 cup white or black sesame seeds, or a combination of both

Directions

1. Toast the coconut in a skillet on medium low heat, stirring frequently, for about four minutes, until the color begins to change to a golden yellow. Remove from the heat and set aside.

2. Cut the cucumbers into noodles using a spiralizer or julienne into long strips. Transfer them to a cutting board or other flat workspace covered with a paper towel. Lightly press another paper towel atop the cucumbers to absorb any excess water before placing them in a large bowl.

3. Julienne the bok choy and add it to the bowl. Toss the vegetables to combine and set aside.

4. Place all the sauce ingredients in a food processor and pulse until smooth. Pour the sauce over the vegetables and toss, coating them evenly. Add the coconut and toss again.

5. Transfer to serving bowls and top each portion with cilantro, scallions, peanuts, and sesame seeds. Serve immediately.

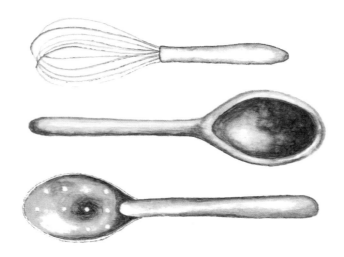

Fall / Winter

Spiced Pumpkin Soup with Chickpeas

Rosemary Potatoes

Pumpkin soup is the quintessential fall food—and for good reason.

If you're looking to warm up with something delicious or to nourish your skin after spending the summer outdoors, cozy up with a bowl of pumpkin soup this fall. Pumpkins aren't just for pies and coffee drinks; they present a nutritionally abundant proposition for savory cooking as well. Here I'm sharing a North African inspired pumpkin soup recipe with seasonal spices, black pepper essential oil, and protein-rich chickpeas that makes a delicious fall meal in a bowl.

The Body in Fall

Fall begins a time of deep inner work that extends through winter. The shifting seasons beckon us. There's a new crispness in the air and deep in the earth the soil microbes are changing. As the days become shorter and colder, our bodies shift as well. These transitional periods offer interesting opportunities to practice listening to the body and to notice how it's relating to the natural world. For example, we might find that we have less energy. The parasympathetic nervous system is more active in the colder months. This is the part of the involuntary nervous system that slows heart rate, increases intestinal and glandular activity, and relaxes the sphincter muscles. Fall is a good time to slow down and allow the body space to begin restoring itself.

If you choose to nurture your body with seasonal food, you might find that you get out of bed with more grace and ease throughout the winter, and even keep a healthy glow going. The light, cooling foods we enjoyed during the summer, some raw or only lightly cooked, are no longer what our bodies need; as we move into fall, we begin to crave warmer, heartier foods.

In the Ayurvedic system, sweet, sour, salty, heavy, moist, oily, and hot foods are recommended in fall, because these foods are believed to work in concert with the body's energies. Generally speaking, think tubers of all sorts with a little healthy fat; warm, whole grains; cooked fruit like apples and bananas; most nuts and seeds; many spices; and if you aren't vegan or vegetarian, meat, eggs, dairy, and seasonal fish. The idea is to keep the body warm, grounded, and well-nourished while it restores itself and builds its defense against winter illnesses.

Pretty Powerful Pumpkins

Each time I pass a pumpkin patch, or even a group of pumpkins assembled in a rustic, fall-themed display at the grocery store, my heart lingers a little. I'm sure I'm not alone, given the number of pumpkin products around each fall. Of course, there are many explanations for our collective pumpkin obsession, ranging from nostalgia to marketing—and from a nutritional standpoint, there's also good reason.

Seasonal foods engage in silent dialogue with the body. Pumpkin and other fall foods contain microbes that support immunity by increasing heat and digestive strength, just what we need to keep us feeling well during this fall. Pumpkin in particular is packed with vitamin A, which boosts cell turnover and nourishes hair, skin, nails, bones, and teeth. After restless, sun-drenched summers, fall foods restore us.

And take note: pumpkin's health benefits extend to its seeds, which are one of the best plant-based sources of zinc, an anti-inflammatory that is also great for hair, skin, and nails. Reserve the seeds and roast them with sea salt and spices, and you'll have a delicious healthy snack to enjoy.

Every fall when my body starts to slow down a little, I remind myself that it's working beautifully. The idea that the body moves through harmonic seasonal cycles with the earth might at first seem a little woo-woo, but with each new study, it becomes uncannily logical. Although I read each new piece of research with appreciation, there's nothing that compares to the feeling of knowing that occurs at both the psychic and physical level when one connects to the rhythm of the earth.

Through seasonal eating, food has the power to open that door. For me, this small act has been life changing, and it's a path that I wholeheartedly encourage everyone to take.

Spiced Pumpkin Soup with Chickpeas

Servings: 4

Ingredients

- 2 tablespoons extra-virgin olive oil, plus more for serving
- 1/2 teaspoon ground caraway seed
- 1/4 teaspoon ground coriander
- 1/4 teaspoon ground cumin
- 1 teaspoon dried red pepper
- 1 teaspoon dried ground mint
- 2 cloves of garlic, smashed with the back of a large knife
- 1/2 teaspoon sea salt, plus more to taste
- 1 pound pumpkin, peeled, seeded, and cut into large chunks
- 2 cups vegetable stock, chicken stock, or water
- 1 cup cooked chickpeas
- 3/4 cup plain Greek yogurt
- 1 drop food grade black pepper essential oil (or 1/4 teaspoon cracked black pepper)
- fresh lemon juice to taste
- a handful of parsley, chopped (for garnish)

Directions

1. Heat the olive oil in a heavy-bottomed soup pan. Add the dried spices (and cracked black pepper, if using it instead of essential oil) and stir until they release fragrance.

2. Add the garlic, pumpkin, and sea salt, and stir, smothering the pumpkin. Add stock or water, raise the heat, and bring to a boil.

3. Immediately lower the heat to a gentle simmer and cook for 10 minutes. Remove from the heat to cool. After the mixture has cooled, transfer it to a blender or food processor and blend to a smooth consistency.

4. Return the soup to the saucepan, stir in the chickpeas and parsley, turn on the heat, and cook until the chickpeas are warm.

5. Meanwhile, put the yogurt in a nonreactive bowl, add black pepper oil, and stir well to combine.

6. Plate soup: top each serving with yogurt, add a squeeze of lemon juice, garnish with parsley, and serve.

Reimagining comfort food starts with the simple yet sustaining potato.

Oh, the poor potato! Once a staple of many diets around the world, it has been unjustly maligned in recent years due to its starchiness, which lands it high on the glycemic index. In actuality, this traditional food comes in degrees of starchiness depending on the variety, and also has a good amount of nutrients. There are documented reports of people living exclusively on potatoes for up to three years. In my mind, the worst thing about them is that they're often ill-prepared, and what ends up on our plates is a soggy shadow of what a potato could be.

A potato can be transformed, seemingly endlessly, by all kinds of methods. Fried, puréed, mashed, baked—they're all delicious when done well. The recipe I'm presenting here is a modern version of the classic roasted potatoes with rosemary; the twist is the inclusion of essential oil. This recipe will elevate the humble potato into a heavenly little parcel that's crispy on the outside and melt-in-your-mouth pillowy on the inside, and the rosemary essential oil adds a new dimension of flavor—and nutrition—to this timeless dish.

Essential Oil Nutrition

Separating foods and their nutrients is not my favorite topic, but the more I learn about the nutritional profile of essential oils, the more intrigued I become. Essential oils are captured, concentrated plant energy—and their nutritional profiles seem to reflect that. Studies place them high on the ORAC (oxygen radical absorbance capacity) scale, a measure of determining a substance's ability to quench free radicals. For example, raw spinach was recently measured at around 1500 units, while studies landed rose essential oil at around 160,000, and clove essential oil at a staggering 1 million plus. Rosemary essential oil comes in around 330. A daily intake between 3,000 and 5,000 units is thought to have a significant impact on plasma and tissue antioxidant capacity. When viewed from a nutritional standpoint, ingesting essential oils is a little like taking vitamin supplements, but with another benefit: flavor.

Eating For Fall

After the sun-drenched energy of summer, fall is a good time to slow down a little and allow the body to restore itself. With flu season on the horizon, it's a vital time to take care in an effort to strengthen immunity. But this can be challenging; the frenetic activity of returning to work and school and the start of the holiday season can interrupt even the most well established self-care rituals. When you haven't found time to go to yoga and it's too cold to enjoy a walk, what you eat becomes more important than ever. During the fall and winter, healthy fats are emphasized in the Ayurvedic diet. They warm the body, assist in the absorption of vitamins and minerals, and moisturize skin from the inside. Additionally, in Ayurveda, potatoes, like other vegetables that grow underground all summer, are generally best during the fall/winter vata season, from November to February. However, their effect on the body varies depending on the type of potato and preparation. I prefer red-skinned potatoes, which are more waxy than starchy, and I always keep the skin on, which is where a lot of the nutrition is.

But enough about nutrition! You won't be thinking about that when these potatoes emerge hot, crispy and fragrant from the oven. And although a recent study confirmed the long-held belief that rosemary improves memory (read about it at http://www.bbc.com/news/magazine-33519453), when you taste these potatoes, you'll know that's not the only reason they're unforgettable.

Rosemary Potatoes

Servings: 6

Ingredients

- 2 pounds small red potatoes, cleaned
- 1/8 cup melted ghee (or butter or oil)
- 2 teaspoons sea salt
- 1 tablespoon minced garlic (about 3 cloves)
- 4 drops organic, therapeutic grade rosemary essential oil (can use fresh/dried instead)
- minced fresh rosemary (optional, for garnish)

Directions

1. Preheat the oven to 400°F. Line a baking sheet with parchment.

2. Quarter the potatoes, leaving the skin on. Place in a bowl and toss with ghee (or butter or oil) and salt, making sure the potatoes are evenly coated.

3. Spread the potatoes onto the baking sheet in a single layer, making sure they have enough space between them to brown. Bake for 45 minutes to 1 hour, flipping twice during cooking to ensure even browning.

4. Remove from the oven, add garlic, and bake for another 5 minutes, until the potatoes are deeply golden and crisp.

5. Remove them from the oven and add rosemary essential oil and rosemary garnish, mixing well. Serve immediately.

Sips

Essential Lemon Peppermint Water

Cranberry Elixir

This refreshing beverage is a bright spot in any day.

Lemons are amazing. What other fruit possesses the power to add an unmatchable zing to a variety of dishes ranging from salad dressing to fish to cake; clean pots and pans; and also alleviate the symptoms of a common cold? I composed this love letter to lemons when I found myself in a hotel room on the other side of the country, nearly defeated by a sinus cold. Instead of asking room service for a lemon with God-knows-what pesticides on it, I did something I'd never done before: I placed a few drops of lemon essential oil in spring water and drank. Instantly uplifted by bright flavor, I was transported out of that stuffy hotel room to a long-ago time when I walked under extravagant trellised lemon trees near the seaside in Sorrento. For a moment, I could taste salty air tinged with lemon blossoms. Then my thoughts were: *Lemon essential oil, where have you been all of my life, and what other amazing powers do you have?* Whole, fresh fruit is a hard act to follow, but lemon essential oil is wonderful in that it's kind of like having a bunch of lemons in my handbag ready to enjoy anytime I'd like.

Lemon isn't the only powerhouse here: peppermint is adaptogenic; it will stimulate or relax the body in order to bring it into homeostasis, or balance. This drink is alkalizing and can be sipped throughout the day. It also encourages oxygen delivery, so it's great before exercise.

I, like many of us, am fascinated by medicinal plants and foods. Maybe it's intuitive, or written into our genetics. After all, in the not too distant past, nature was our pharmacy. Whatever the reasons, I developed quite an affection for Samantha Wright's lemon peppermint water recipe, which I'm including here. It's incredibly refreshing, and each time I drink it, I'm reminded that when life gives you lemons, you can always brighten things up with a few drops of lemon essential oil.

Essential Lemon Peppermint Water

Servings: 4

Ingredients

- 1/2 gallon spring water
- 2 drops each peppermint and lemon oils
- 1 tablespoon pure unheated honey

Directions

1. Mix all ingredients in a glass or other nonreactive container. (Mix well; the honey will help the oil disperse through the water.)

The bitterness of the fresh cranberries is balanced by the orange and stevia in this healthy drink.

zesty &
detoxifying

Would you like to clean up from the inside out or give your immune system a boost? Cranberries are packed full of detoxifying nutrients that can guard your body against disease. Here I'll teach you how to harness their nutritional powers by creating a drink that will give you a huge dose of protective plant elements.

Cranberries are in season throughout fall and winter. You'll get the most nutrients from the fresh fruit, so pick some up while they're in season; this delicious, healthy drink will have you missing them come spring.

Why Cranberries?

The humble little cranberry is an underrated superfood. It contains a good amount of vitamin C, but there's much more to its outstanding nutritional profile. It outranks nearly every fruit and vegetable in antioxidants, including strawberries, spinach, broccoli, red grapes, raspberries, and cherries. One cup of cranberries contains 8,983 antioxidants, second only to blueberries. Antioxidants protect the body by neutralizing free radicals that are generated during normal metabolic processes, and as a result of exposure to environmental toxins like ozone, cigarette smoke, air pollutants, industrial chemicals, and x-rays. An excess amount of free radicals creates

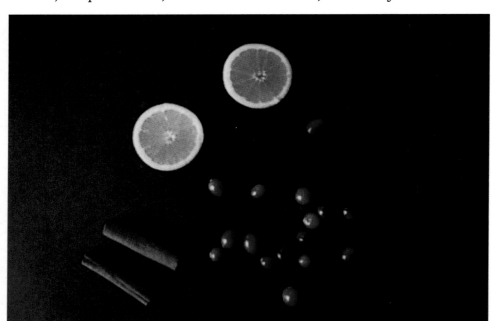

oxidative stress in the body, which can trigger a number of diseases and accelerate aging. Cranberries are particularly rich in phenols, potent antioxidants that are more powerful than those found in most vitamin supplements. Along with all of those great antioxidants, cranberries contain anthocyanins and proanthocyanidins, enigmatic polyphenols that give them the ability to reduce inflammation and prevent harmful bacteria from getting cozy in our bodies.

Beyond the Sauce

Have you ever tasted a fresh, raw cranberry? The first time I popped one in my mouth, I immediately withered under a small shock of bitterness. Consequently, I, like so many other home cooks, relegated them to a single purpose for the next 20 years—sauce. Fresh cranberries create a sauce that surpasses the canned jellied version in every way, but there are other delicious ways to enjoy them, too. They're great in sweet tarts, paired with ricotta on crostini, in braised cabbage, and in drinks. Blending cranberries into a drink has one distinct advantage over other ways you can eat them: their nutritional value is most accessible when the fruit is eaten uncooked.

You won't have to worry about excessive bitterness with the cranberry detox elixir I'm sharing ere. In it, cranberries' sharpness is balanced by the sweetness of oranges, cinnamon, and stevia, roducing a zesty but balanced and satisfying drink.

Cinnamon bark essential oil is a must here over the dried spice, both for its texture and erfumey flavor. Also, just like with cranberries, ingesting essential oil unheated means all of its utritional goodness is preserved.

Stevia is derived from the stevia plant, a sweet herb that has been eaten in South America for ɩore than 1500 years. The sweetness of stevia products varies, but one manufacturer describes the lant's leaves as 20 times as sweet as sugar. Despite this profound sweetness, many people find tevia has a bitter or menthol flavor, especially when consumed in generous amounts. This weet/bitter profile both harmonizes with and lifts the flavor of cranberries in this drink. When uying liquid stevia, choose one that's pure and free of alcohol, artificial colors, flavors, and reservatives.

The abundant fall harvest, with all of those wonderful squashes, apples, and citrus fruits, is nticipated by many of us, but by the time January rolls around, it's not uncommon to begin to ream of spring. Maybe this is due to the unsettled human spirit, or simply because we've been nowed upon one too many times by that point. Whatever the reason, it's delightful to realize the ɩagical little cranberry is there in the middle of all of that. Cranberries' remarkable phytonutrients kely evolved together with their resilience. Although they're dainty and rather thin-skinned, they, ke the rest of their fall/winter friends, are remarkably sturdy. If stored well, they'll hold up in your efrigerator for up to two months according to a number of sources, but don't leave them waiting for ɔng. Cranberries will not only add a wonderful tart flavor and beautiful ruby red color to your ʋinter table, they'll also impart you with some of the best nutrients around.

Cranberry Elixir

Servings: 1

Ingredients

- 1 cup fresh cranberries
- 1 cup purified water
- 1 Valencia orange, seeds removed and juiced
- 5 drops liquid stevia
- 4 drops food grade cinnamon bark essential oil

Directions

1. Rinse the cranberries and place them in a food processor or blender. Add water, orange juice, and stevia. Blend on high for 4 minutes.

2. Place 1 tablespoon of water into a glass and add the cinnamon bark essential oil. Using a nonreactive utensil, stir to combine. Add the cranberry mixture to the glass and mix again. Serve immediately.

Sweets

Peanut Butter Chocolate Chip Nice Cream

Chocolate Avocado Mousse

Delicious dessert doesn't have to be unhealthy.

If you're looking for an easy way to have a delicious, healthy, homemade dessert, I've got the scoop for you. And although it's not *exactly* ice cream, its flavor lets it stand on its own.

"Nice cream" is a cool, creamy, vegan treat that employs a trick the whole world should know about: bananas can transform into ice cream. The first time I pulsed frozen bananas in a food processor, I was surprised—and delighted—by the result: rich, perfectly sweet without any added sugar, and very much like ice cream. And, outside of the freezing time, the entire thing took about five minutes to put together. Pulsed bananas provide a base to which nuts, chocolate, and fruit blend beautifully. Here I'm sharing one of my favorite "nice cream" recipes, which, in addition to bananas, involves a little peanut butter, a hint of cinnamon bark essential oil, and chunks of dark chocolate.

You'll need a strong food processor or blender to aerate the bananas. I prefer a food processor but once when I used a small one for this, it blew out; the larger version has worked without fail. Although frozen bananas can be challenging for some machines, they melt quickly. It might take you a few times to get the texture you want, but the result will always be delicious. As you pulse the bananas, you'll witness them transform into a soft serve like texture. If you're into that, as I am, serve immediately. However, if you'd like a more solid dessert, place the nice cream in the freezer for another three hours or more before serving.

A Dairy Alternative

Although I still love good dairy products, there are many reasons I eat less of them these days. Even at the best ice cream shops and bakeries, I can't help but wonder what exactly I'm eating. If you're anything like me, your appetite has been diminished by stories about ultra-pasteurized milk, GMOs, pesticides, hormones, and the many mysterious ingredients on food labels that aren't actually foods. Or maybe you're one of the seemingly ever-growing crowd who doesn't digest dairy products well. And of course, there are the environmental concerns associated with dairy production. A recent study by an independent research company hired by an environmentally-friendly ice cream manufacturer found that one pint of their ice cream added up to two pounds of CO_2 emissions into the atmosphere, equivalent to driving two miles in a medium-sized car. Most of this number was due to the use of dairy ingredients, as opposed to packaging or manufacturing.

One of my oldest friends and I are bonded through food. It's been this way since we were girls. It was she who made me a raw milk alchemist. With the help of a local dairy farmer, a stand mixer, and just a few sips of whisky, she taught me how to make ice cream. For most people, dairy's transformational powers are at once mysterious and awe-inspiring. My friend and I keep our memories like jewels, but these days, more often than not, we opt for "nice cream," and, dare I say, we're just as happy.

Peanut Butter Chocolate Chip Nice Cream

Servings: 6 (about 3 cups)

Ingredients

- 3 large ripe bananas
- 3-1/2 tablespoons crunchy peanut butter
- 2 drops food grade cinnamon bark essential oil (or 1/2 teaspoon dried cinnamon)
- 1/4 teaspoon fine sea salt
- 1-1/2 ounces dark chocolate chips or chopped dark chocolate
- chopped peanuts for garnish (optional)

Directions

1. Peel and cut the bananas into coin-shaped pieces. Put the pieces in an airtight container and place in the freezer overnight, or for at least three hours.

2. When you're ready to assemble the ice cream, measure out the peanut butter in a glass or other nonreactive bowl. Add the cinnamon bark essential oil and mix well. (This step is to dilute the essential oil and prevent it from reacting to the plastic food processor bowl).

3. After the bananas are frozen, transfer them to a food processor or strong blender and pulse. While the bananas change texture from crumbly to smooth and creamy, you

might need to scrape down the bowl periodically. The bananas should reach a creamy texture in about 1 minute.

4. Add the peanut butter/cinnamon bark essential oil mixture and sea salt to the bananas and pulse until well combined, about another 30 seconds.

5. Transfer the mixture to a bowl, add the chocolate, and mix until combined.

6. If you like a soft serve texture, serve immediately. If you prefer a more solid texture, transfer to an airtight container and freeze until solid (3 hours or more). Upon serving, top each portion with chopped peanuts, if desired.

indulgent &

smooth

This perfectly guilt-free indulgence has a secret ingredient for extra creaminess.

To create a delicious, nutritionally significant treat, trying adding avocados to your chocolate mousse. If you've never tasted chocolate avocado mousse, you just might find that you love it; and for those of you who are practiced with it, I think you'll appreciate the unique, slightly floral flavor in this recipe. An added benefit is that it takes about ten minutes to put together.

This dish is the perfect conclusion to an indulgent, celebratory feast. I love celebrating, with all of its festivities, friends & family, and food. But frequently indulging in rich, "special occasion" meals full of industrial dairy leaves me running on my last energy reserves and regretting it. American holiday food is cream-heavy, from pumpkin pie to mashed potatoes, and although real ultured cream is incredibly healthy for many of us, the majority of the foods we encounter are filled with the type of dairy that's toxic to our bodies. As if that isn't bad enough, many of these foods are loaded with processed sugar and unhealthy fat. But not chocolate avocado mousse.

I love sweets, so I'm always looking to make them as healthy as possible. One day when I was without raw cream for chocolate mousse, I reluctantly gave avocados a try. I was categorically opposed to sweetening avocados and mixing them with chocolate, but after the first taste, I got over it. The result was delicious, luscious, and even kid-approved. Avocados are packed with vitamins, minerals, and healthy fat. Use good quality dark chocolate and unsweetened cocoa and you'll have a nutrient dense dessert. Melted chocolate is a must—it creates a depth that goes hand in hand with avocado's richness. After a few recipe tests, I added a drop of black pepper essential oil. In this form, black pepper loses its heat and displays a floral side that works nicely with chocolate, vanilla, and avocado. Black pepper essential oil offers an interesting opportunity to know this common spice in a new way.

When I first heard about chocolate avocado mousse, I thought, really? During the course of my life, I've witnessed the ascendance of the avocado. When I was growing up in Southern California, avocados were plenty. It wasn't uncommon for neighbors to share fruit that was falling from trees in their yards. I had no idea that the rest of the world was largely bereft of avocados until I went away to college. Of course, that's all changed in recent years due to trade agreements and marketing. Now avocados are available pretty much year-round in most of the U.S. Consequently, the avocado has become the subject of innumerable Instagram homages and appears on everything from toast to t-shirts. All of this craziness led me to doubt chocolate avocado mousse as just another farfetched marketing ploy, but I stand humbly corrected. With this recipe, the avocado transcends another category—dessert. In doing so, it yet again makes the world more of an unapologetically delicious place.

Chocolate Avocado Mousse

Servings: 4-6

Ingredients

- 1/2 cup maple syrup
- 1 tablespoon pure vanilla extract
- 1 drop food grade black pepper essential oil
- 4 very ripe avocados, pitted and peeled
- 1/2 cup unsweetened cocoa powder
- 1/4 teaspoon sea salt
- 4 ounces bittersweet chocolate (or 1/2 cup chocolate chips)

garnish (optional)

- shaved chocolate
- nuts (pistachios, walnuts, or almonds work well)

Directions

1. Measure maple syrup and vanilla into a glass or other nonreactive bowl. Add black pepper essential oil, stir to combine, and set aside.

2. Place the avocados, cocoa powder, sea salt, and vanilla in a food processor and set aside.

3. Cut the chocolate into small pieces, and place in a double boiler (a bowl over a small saucepan of water). Bring to a weak simmer over low heat, stirring the chocolate until melted.

4. Add melted chocolate to the food processor basket and blend until well combined, scraping down the sides of the bowl as necessary. Add maple syrup/vanilla/essential oil mixture and process until smooth.

5. Spoon chocolate mousse into serving bowls, cover, and refrigerate for at least three hours or up to one day. Garnish with chocolate shavings and nuts, if using, and serve.

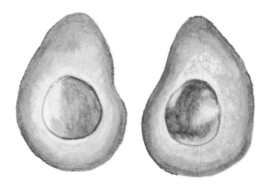

Watch Out for These 8 Oils

By Anna Marija Helt, PhD

Before you start experimenting with other essential oils in your cooking, do your research and make sure they're completely safe for human consumption. And to be on the conservative side, we recommend completely avoiding these eight essential oils.

What essential oils are in your medicine cabinet? Being commercially available doesn't mean that an essential oil is safe to have around the house. Oral overdosing of toxic oils is the cause of very serious outcomes like liver or kidney damage, convulsions, coma and, in multiple cases, death. But even low oral doses or topical application can be a problem with some oils. Most of us don't ingest essential oils in large amounts, but what happens with regular, lower dose use of oils containing high levels of toxic components? For the most part, it's a big unknown.

That said, most oils on the market are generally safe with reasonable usage. This means that there are lots of great oils to use instead of those that can potentially cause problems. Here are eight commercially available oils with the potential to cause problems, along with some safer substitutes for them.

Sources for this article:

Tisserand, R. and R. Young (2014) Essential Oil Safety, 2nd Edition. Elsevier, Churchill, Livingstone.

Mills, S. and K. Bone (2005) The essential guide to herbal safety. Elsevier, Churchill, Livingstone.

Watch out for: Black Mustard (*Brassica nigra*)

Mustard essential oil has been used as a circulatory and digestive stimulant, as well as for pain and infections. But it's Hot with a capital H! Ever tried a mustard plaster with the seed or powder? Ouch, even this can burn you!

Why to avoid Black Mustard

- Strong skin and mucus membrane irritant. Blistering possible.
- Inhalation very irritating to respiratory tract and eyes.

Chemical(s) responsible

- Allyl isothiocyanate, which is also in horseradish essential oil.

Use instead of Black Mustard

- Digestion, circulation, and achy muscles—Rosemary (*Rosmarinus officinalis*)
- Pain or infection—Lavender (*Lavandula angustifolia*), frankincense (*Boswellia* species)   and/or sweet marjoram (*Origanum majorana*)

Watch out for: Wintergreen (*Gaultheria procumbens*)

A popular oil, with a sweet, candy-like scent, it's used as a muscle liniment and for joint pain.

Why to avoid Wintergreen

- Oral overdosing may lead to convulsions, coma, and possibly death.
- Ingestion of about a teaspoon or more has been fatal in children. Its appealing scent may have tempted them to drink it.

- Topical preparations (creams, etc.) have resulted in toxicity, though many use wintergreen topically for pain without any apparent issues.

- Contains over 90% methyl salicylate, which can impact the nervous system, circulatory system, liver, and kidneys.

- Pain—Frankincense, sweet marjoram, and/or lavender
- Muscle liniment—Rosemary (*Rosmarinus officinalis*)

Watch out for: Parsleyseed (*Petroselenium cripsum*)

Parsley leaf reigns in the kitchen and is a super healthy addition to the diet when not overdone. Parsleyseed oil is from the same plant and has been used for digestive and menstrual cramping, menstrual cycle irregularities, musculoskeletal pain, urinary tract issues, and for treating viral infections.

- Fatalities have occurred from accidental or deliberate ingestion of parsleyseed oil at high doses.
- Liver, kidney, and digestive tract toxicity is possible in people.
- The German Commission E Monograph for parsleyseed oil concludes that its benefits don't outweigh the risks.

- Parsley apiole: 11 to over 60% of the essential oil.

- Cramping—German chamomile (*Matricaria recutita*)
- Musculoskeletal pain—Lavender, frankincense, and/or marjoram

- Menstrual cycle support—Rose (*Rosa* species), Geranium (*Pelargonium* species) or clary sage (*Salvia sclarea*)
- Viral infection—Lavender

Watch out for: Calamus (*Acorus calamus*)

I have calamus root in my apothecary, but not the essential oil, which is used in perfumery, for memory support, for nervous tics, and for musculoskeletal pain.

Why to avoid Calamus

- The purified essential oil may be a liver toxin.
- Potential for toxicity from skin absorption has led to only very dilute amounts recommended for topical use (0.2% or 2 drops per every 1000 drops of carrier).
- Cancer promoting in rats, though rat experiments don't always translate to people.

Chemical(s) responsible

- Commercial calamus essential oil is often from an Asian variety that contains the potential liver toxin beta-asarone in high amounts.
- Methyl eugenol may be present as well, and is toxic to the liver in small amounts.

Use instead of Calamus

- Musculoskeletal pain—Frankincense, lavender, sweet marjoram
- Nervous system tics—Lavender, frankincense, chamomile, tangerine
- Memory—Rosemary

Watch out for: Pennyroyal (*Mentha pulegium*)

As a plant, pennyroyal has a long history of use for a variety of health issues: Cold/flu, digestion, lack of menses, fever, and as an abortifacient. The oil is sold for similar uses and has generated a notorious reputation.

Why to avoid Pennyroyal

- Can cause liver and kidney damage, as well as seizures, with high oral dosing (~1 teaspoon).
- Has caused multiple fatalities.
- Oil toxicity has been observed even in small quantities.
- The tea has also caused toxicity.
- Topical over-usage as flea repellent has resulted in canine deaths.

Chemical(s) responsible

- Pugelone, present in high quantities in the oil.

Use instead of Pennyroyal

- Indigestion—Chamomile, lavender, sweet marjoram
- Cold/flu—Lavender, sweet marjoram
- Menstrual cycle support—Rose, geranium or clary sage

Watch out for: Tansy (*Tanacetum vulgare*)

A beautiful plant that may be best to just look at! Tansy oil has been used for worms, to bring on delayed menses, as an antiseptic, as an anti-inflammatory and as antihistamine.

Why to avoid Tansy

- Can cause digestive tract inflammation, vomiting, liver toxicity, convulsions, rapid breathing and irregular heartbeat.

- Oral overdosing has caused fatalities.

- External use can cause toxicity.

- Even the tea has shown toxicity.

Chemical(s) responsible

- Thujone, a neurotoxin—Tansy essential oil is almost half thujone.

Use instead of Tansy

- Worms—Garlic cloves

- Antiseptic—Lavender

- Menstrual cycle support—Rose, geranium, or clary sage

- Inflammation—Chamomile, frankincense

- Anti-histamine—Chamomile

Watch out for: Sage (*Salvia officinalis*)

Yup, plain old garden sage. I frequently use sage tea and tincture for myself and my clients. **Just not the essential oil.** Sage is used for too many things to list...digestion, brain function, infection, and more!

Why to avoid Sage

- Folks have had seizures after ingesting 12 or more drops of sage oil.

- One of my aromatherapy teachers didn't even like to use the oil as an inhalant for folks already having any sort of nervous system issue (tics, seizures, anxiety, etc.).

Chemical(s) responsible

- Thujone, a neurotoxin—Sage oil averages around 30-50% thujone, with levels sometimes close to 70%.

- The tea! The tincture! These are great choices!

Watch out for: Cedar (*Thuja* species)

Cedar is used for bronchitis, menstrual cycle support, skin issues, and musculoskeletal pain, as room disinfectants and to terminate pregnancies. Cedar has also been used for grounding. Note that these are from completely different species than oils such as Atlas cedarwood.

- Convulsions have resulted, even from ingestion of a 0.1% dilution (1 drop per 1000 drops of carrier) of northern white cedar (T. occidentalis).
- Reproductive effects—Uterine stimulatory activity, and may suppress ovulation.
- Skin reactions and contact allergies have occurred.

- Thujone, a neurotoxin—High in both oils, though higher in western red cedar.

- Grounding—Vetiver
- Room disinfectant—Rosemary
- Menstrual cycle support—Rose, geranium, or clary sage
- Skin issues—German Chamomile
- Musculoskeletal pain—Frankincense, lavender, sweet marjoram
- Bronchitis—Lavender, Roman chamomile (*Anthemis nobilis*)

b a s m a t i

Recipes & Photos

Shiraz Leyva

Editors

Jen Wilson

Ursula Squire

Paintings by Jenna Horenn

basmati

Growing your own herbs and veggies?
We have an ebook to help: *Organic and Sustainable Home Gardening.*

Making your own natural, organic beauty products?
Discover new recipes in our *Natural, Homemade Beauty* ebook!

Learn more about the ancient tradition of Ayurveda in our book, *Ayurveda: An Introductory Look.*

Read more about essential oils on our website, www.basmati.com.
If you have questions about essential oils, submit a question on our practitioner forum.

You can also find a practitioner or a yoga studio near you on our website, as well as lots of organic, sustainable, and vegan products in our specially curated shop.

Made in the USA
Middletown, DE
15 June 2020